Then and Now

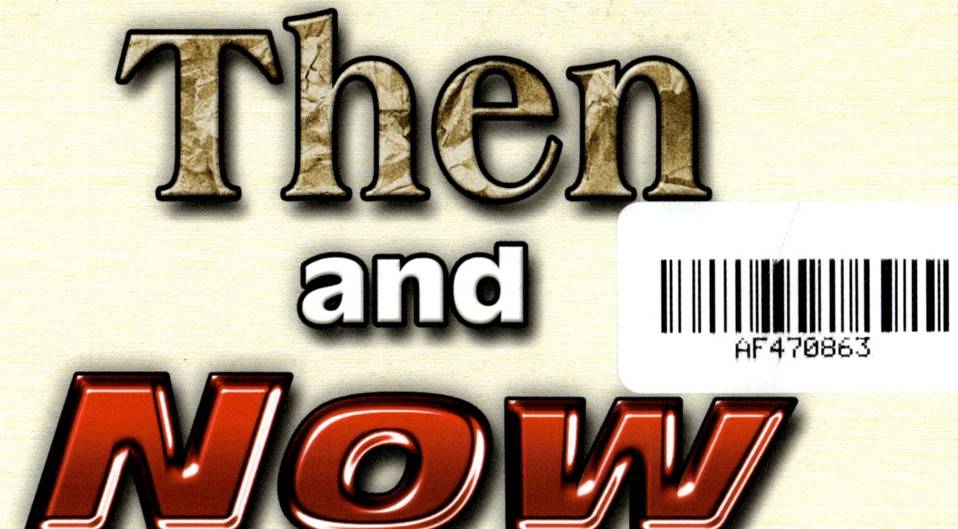

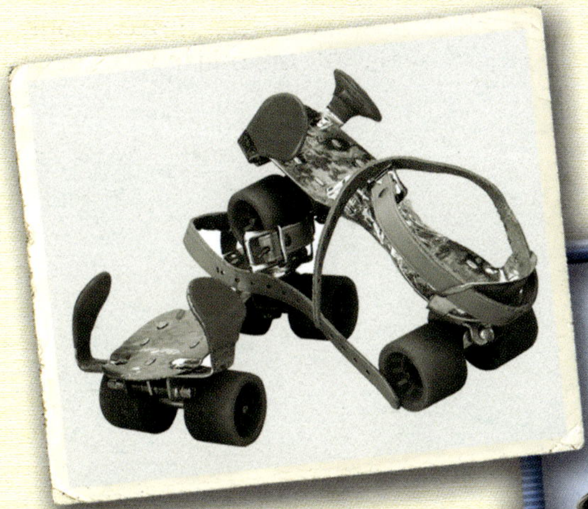

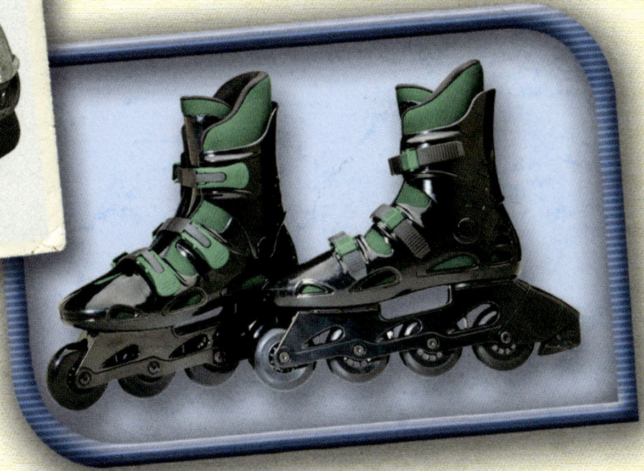

Claire Llewellyn

RIGBY

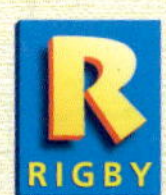

Things Change

Every day we use things like cars, computers and telephones.
These things were first made a long time ago.

What did they look like long ago?
How have they changed?

Cars Then

Old cars did not go very fast.
They had seats for just two people.
The seats were very hard.

Cars Now

New cars go very fast.
They have seats for many people.
Now the seats are soft.

Telephones Then

Old telephones were very big.
They were always black.
The numbers were on a dial.

Telephones Now

New telephones are very little.
They now come in many colours.
The numbers are on buttons now.

Watches Then

Old watches had a big face.
They had hands to tell the time.
People put the watches in their pockets.

Watches Now

Many new watches have a small face.
Some just have numbers to tell the time.
Now people wear watches on their arm.

Televisions Then

Old televisions had little screens.
They showed black and white pictures.
The first televisions had dials to make
them work.

Televisions Now

Many new televisions have big screens.
Now they show pictures in colour.
They have buttons to make them work.

Computers Then

Old computers were very big.
They did not have a screen.
Old computers did not work very fast.

Computers Now

New computers are small.
They have a colour screen.
New computers work very fast.

Then

How have these things changed over time?

Now

Index